Ancient Indians

of the
Southwest

BY DAVID GRANT NOBLE

SOUTHWEST PARKS AND MONUMENTS ASSOCIATION

Who were the first people who lived in the Southwest?

1 We call them Paleo-Indians and they appeared toward the end of the last Ice Age – at least twelve thousand years ago. They were the first Americans. The word *paleo* (PAY-leo) means ancient or old.

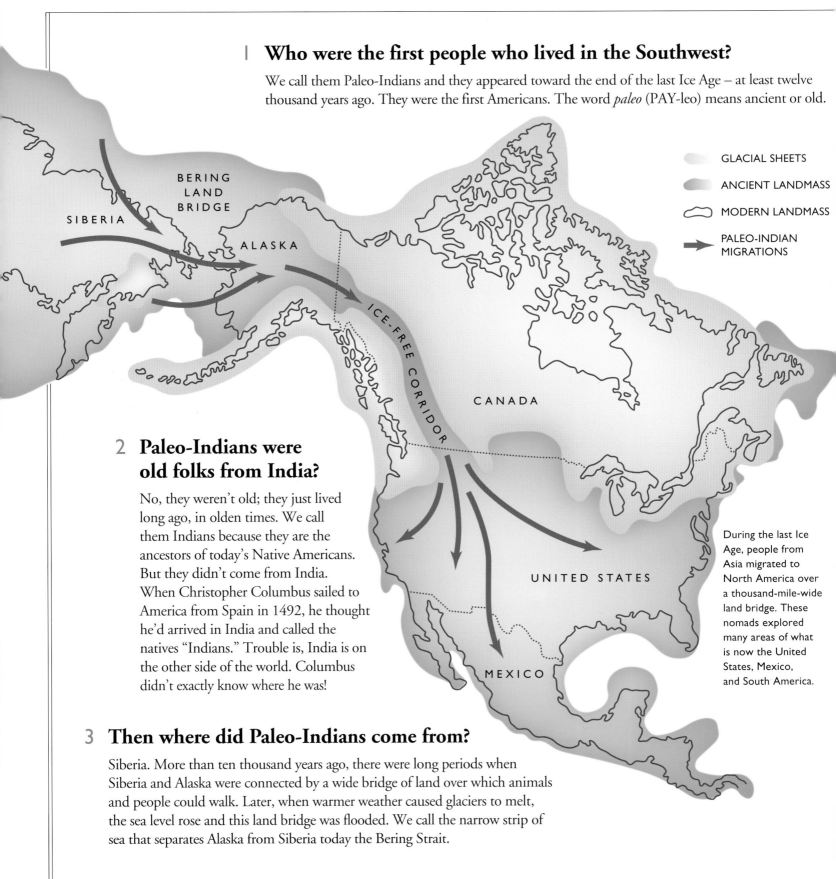

GLACIAL SHEETS

ANCIENT LANDMASS

MODERN LANDMASS

PALEO-INDIAN MIGRATIONS

SIBERIA

BERING LAND BRIDGE

ALASKA

ICE-FREE CORRIDOR

CANADA

UNITED STATES

MEXICO

During the last Ice Age, people from Asia migrated to North America over a thousand-mile-wide land bridge. These nomads explored many areas of what is now the United States, Mexico, and South America.

2 Paleo-Indians were old folks from India?

No, they weren't old; they just lived long ago, in olden times. We call them Indians because they are the ancestors of today's Native Americans. But they didn't come from India. When Christopher Columbus sailed to America from Spain in 1492, he thought he'd arrived in India and called the natives "Indians." Trouble is, India is on the other side of the world. Columbus didn't exactly know where he was!

3 Then where did Paleo-Indians come from?

Siberia. More than ten thousand years ago, there were long periods when Siberia and Alaska were connected by a wide bridge of land over which animals and people could walk. Later, when warmer weather caused glaciers to melt, the sea level rose and this land bridge was flooded. We call the narrow strip of sea that separates Alaska from Siberia today the Bering Strait.

4 How could anyone walk all the way from Asia to Arizona?

Paleo-Indians were nomads, and they walked everywhere. In those days, the only way to travel was by foot.

If you walked fifteen miles a day every day for six months, you'd cover almost three thousand miles (which would be like walking from the coast of California to the coast of Virginia). But the nomads were in no hurry. Over many centuries, they followed herds of big animals, such as mammoths, southward along the edge of glaciers or down the coast. When they wandered into what we now call the Southwest, the climate was cooler and wetter. You would have seen large spruce and fir forests, sparkling clear lakes, and lush grasslands.

Parts of the Southwest's desert country may have looked like this during the Ice Age.

The bones of over 400 bison killed for food almost ten thousand years ago by Paleo-Indians.

5 What is a mammoth?

A gigantic hairy elephant that became extinct about eight thousand years ago. Other large animals lived in North America then, too – ancient species of camels and bison, and giant sloths. We have found evidence of them in fossilized bones, and some years ago a frozen mammoth was discovered in Alaska. Meat from its carcass was flown to New York City and served at a dinner for the Explorers' Club.

6 How did they catch such big animals?

One way was for a group of hunters to hide along the edge of a pond and wait for a mammoth to come to drink or wallow. When it waded out in the muddy shallows, the hunters would spring out, surround it, and thrust in their spears.

7 Then what would they do?

Probably celebrate – no worries about food for a while. With their sharp knives made from stone, like flint or chert, Paleo-Indians cut out hunks of meat to roast over a fire – it was an Ice Age cookout! They also cracked open the leg bones and scooped out the marrow, a rich and nutritious food.

9 Where did they stay at night?

Caves made excellent shelters, but they often had to sleep out in the open. They probably made tents from animal skins.

8 Did Paleo-Indians look like us?

Yes, although none have ever been found, say, frozen in an iceberg, so we don't know for sure. We do know that human beings have looked pretty much the same for over fifty thousand years, even though the way we live has changed a lot.

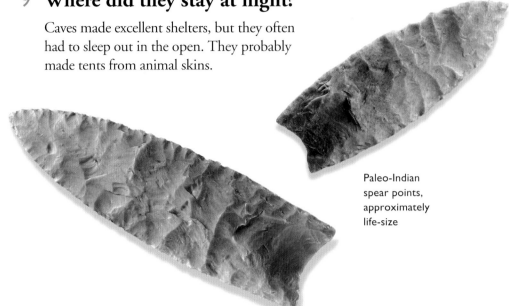

Paleo-Indian spear points, approximately life-size

Hair style and clothing greatly alter how we look. These two pictures are of the same Navajo boy, Tom Toslino. The top one was taken in 1885 when he was sent to a boarding school in Pennsylvania. The bottom one was taken three years later.

10 How do we know Paleo-Indians really existed?

Mainly because we find *artifacts,* such as spear points or stone knives. When these tools are discovered, scientists called *archeologists* come to investigate. Like detectives, they study all the evidence. Paleo-Indians made their spear points in a distinctive style that trained archeologists recognize.

11 Who found the first evidence of Paleo-Indians?

George McJunkin, a cowboy in Folsom, New Mexico. In 1925, he was riding his horse along a stream bed when he spotted some very large bones eroding out of the bank. They belonged to a long-extinct species of bison. Suspecting that his discovery might be important, he reported it. Later, when archeologists studied the site, they found spear points lying among the bison bones, proving that the animal had been killed by humans.

George McJunkin, who discovered th famous Folsom sit in New Mexico.

Logs of stone found lying in the desert today are proof that huge trees grew here when the climate was cooler and wetter. This picture is of Petrified Forest National Park in Arizona.

2 What happened to the Paleo-Indians?

That's kind of a mystery. By eight thousand years ago the climate had grown warmer and drier in the Southwest, more like it is today, and this caused changes in vegetation. Many plants that mammoths and other big game browsed died off and soon the animals became extinct.

As for the nomads, many probably drifted out to the Great Plains where smaller animals like buffalo and antelope grazed. Others stayed where they were and ate whatever foods were available.

13 So, first there were Paleo-Indians, and then there were... ?

Archaic (ar-KAY-ick) people. Guess what *archaic* means . . . right, ancient or old. But, not as old as paleo. Archaic people appeared in the Southwest after Paleo-Indians, about eight thousand years ago.

A few southwestern Indians were still living as hunter-gatherers as late as 1870. These Paiute women are gathering seeds in baskets. Their clothes are made of deerskin.

14 What were Archaic people like?

They were nomadic, too. They traveled around in small bands hunting game and gathering various wild plants for food. For this reason we call them *hunter-gatherers.*

Archaic people hunted animals such as deer, rabbits, and squirrels and collected seeds, nuts, and berries.

A stone pestle used by Archaic Indians to pound seeds into flour

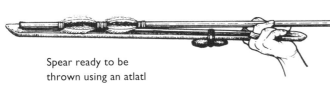
Indian rice grass

15 What were some of the hunter-gatherers' favorite foods?

They liked Indian rice grass and sunflower seeds. Rice grass grows in clumps and produces round brown seeds in early summer. They would shake the seeds into a basket to carry back to camp. Pine nuts, from the pinyon tree, were also a favorite. They picked cactus fruit, gathered greens such as purslane, and dug up wild onions. They fished, caught ducks in large nets, and even ate grasshoppers, crickets, and insect larvae.

Prickly pear cactus in fruit

Pinyon nuts ready to harvest

Spear ready to be thrown using an atlatl

17 What did they use to hunt animals?

Archaic hunters had a device called a spear thrower, or *atlatl*. It's a flattened wooden stick about two feet long with a hand grip at one end and notch at the other. To use it, you grasp the handle and place the end of a short spear in the notch. Then you cock it over your shoulder and throw. With an atlatl, an expert hunter can throw a spear with great force and bring down a deer at a distance of a hundred feet or more. Hunters all over the world used them.

16 They actually ate insects?

Sure, it may seem strange to us today, but insects are highly nutritious – a good source of protein. They can be dried and ground into powder and added to soup.

Grasshoppers were a source of food. Maybe children had fun catching them!

Ancient Indians ate rodents, including Harris's antelope squirrels.

Sometimes stone chips lying on the ground are all that is left today around ancient campsites.

18 Where did hunter-gatherers live?

All over the countryside. It depended on which plants were ready to harvest in what season and where they could find good hunting or fishing. In winter, they usually camped in the lowlands where it was warmer. In summer, they would move to higher elevations where it was cooler. Like Paleo-Indians, Archaic people often stayed in caves for shelter from the rain and wind. They also built lodges of sticks and brush. Of course, in fair weather they probably slept out in the open beneath the stars.

A prehistoric Indian basket

9 What do you find at Archaic campsites today?

Mostly stones – flat stones for grinding seeds, burned stones used in cooking, and stone flakes left over from making tools.

Since pottery hadn't been invented yet, Archaic people cooked with baskets, which they wove tight enough to hold water. Baskets couldn't withstand fire, though, so to boil their stews, they dropped in heated stones.

20 What did they do besides hunt, gather, and travel?

Like all people, they made art. In the Southwest, they are known for the powerful human-like figures they painted on cliff walls. After thousands of years, some of these paintings are still clearly visible today. Some striking examples are in the lower Grand Canyon and in remote areas of Canyonlands National Park.

Archaic Indians painted these mysterious figures on the side of a canyon more than twenty-five hundred years ago. Some are more than five feet tall.

What happened to Archaic people in the Southwest?

About three thousand years ago, many hunter-gatherers began to change their wandering way of life. They began planting corn, building houses, and living in small villages. They became the Southwest's first farmers.

22 Then there were no more hunter-gatherers?

Actually, some did continue to roam the West. In 1776, Spanish explorers met hunter-gatherers in Utah and traded with them for fish to eat. The Utes, who live in Colorado and Utah today, were hunter-gatherers until they acquired horses from Europeans in the seventeenth and eighteenth centuries. And Paiute Indians continued their nomadic lifestyle until the mid-1800s when cattle ranchers and settlers took over their territories, forcing the Paiutes to move to a series of small reservations north of the Grand Canyon.

A few hunter-gatherers still exist in the world – in the Kalahari Desert in South Africa, for example, and in Australia. Until recent times, Eskimos were hunter-gatherers, too.

23 How did the farmers learn to grow corn?

Indians in southern Mexico had been growing it for thousands of years. Even corn had an ancestor, a wild grass called *teosinte* whose seeds once were gathered for food. Word probably traveled by way of traders about seeds that could be planted and made to grow.

Eugene Sekaquaptewa, a Hopi farmer in Arizona, growing corn in the traditional way

24 Is it easy to grow corn?

It takes a lot of work, especially in the desert. Unlike wild seeds, corn must be planted by people in order to sprout, and young plants need almost daily attention. People need to cultivate, water, weed, and protect their gardens from rodents and rabbits. Archaic people learned how to do this, and since it was difficult to tend gardens and be nomads at the same time, they began living in one place.

Archaeologists often find well-preserved corn cobs in prehistoric sites.

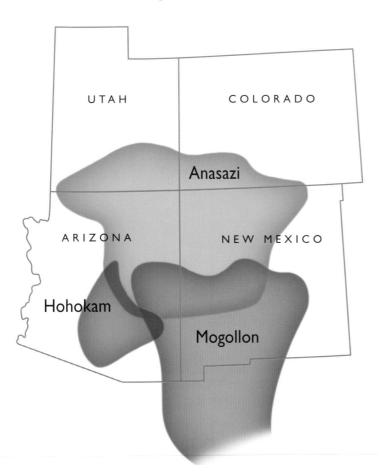

UTAH

COLORADO

Anasazi

ARIZONA

NEW MEXICO

Hohokam

Mogollon

25 Who were these farmers?

Archeologists believe that Archaic people were the ancestors of three groups of farming people who followed them: the *Mogollon* (MUGGY-own), the *Hohokam* (HO-ho-kam), and the *Anasazi* (Ana-SA-zee).

Many Mogollon people lived in the hill country of what is now southwestern New Mexico and southeastern Arizona. The Hohokam lived in the Sonoran Desert areas of southern Arizona. The Anasazi covered the widest area and lived in parts of Arizona, Colorado, New Mexico, and Utah.

26 What kind of tools did the Mogollon have?

They used wooden digging sticks and stone hoes to cultivate their fields. They also had stone hammers and axes. How long do you think it would take to cut down a pine tree with an eight-inch diameter trunk using a stone axe? Less than thirty minutes! Sometimes you find grooves rubbed into cliffs where prehistoric people sharpened their axes.

A stone hoe, *left*, and an axe with a wooden handle

27 What's prehistoric?

Everything that occurred before people started writing and recording what was happening around them. Since ancient North American Indians did not have writing, they passed on knowledge by word of mouth.

28 Did the Mogollon Indians hunt, too?

Yes, a lot. An amazing discovery in 1960 by archeologists Marjorie Lambert and Richard Ambler showed just how much time they must have dedicated to hunting. Marjorie and Richard were excavating the floor of a cave in southwestern New Mexico when they found an extraordinary hunting net. It was 150 feet long, 5 feet wide, and was woven out of human hair! It dated to around 1,000 years ago.

Hunters may have staked this net flat just above the ground so that animals, like rabbits and turkeys, would get their legs tangled up in the webbing.

Large hunting net woven from human hair

29 Where did the Mogollon live?

All southwestern farmers first lived in pit houses. They dug round or oval pits in the ground, lined the sides with stone slabs, and built walls and a roof of branches and grass. They smeared mud on the outside walls and piled dirt on the roof for insulation.

To enter their pit houses, they crawled on their hands and knees through an entryway. A hearth in the floor provided warmth and the smoke escaped through a hole in the ceiling. These dwellings were snug and warm in cold weather.

Partially reconstructed pit house at Mesa Verde

Mimbres bowls are famous for their imaginative paintings.

30 What else did the Mogollon people do?

One group of early Mogollon we call the Mimbres (MIM-brays), are well-known today for the beautiful pottery bowls they made. When Mimbres people died, their relatives and friends carefully buried them in a grave with a bowl placed over their head. Potters decorated these bowls with pictures of people, animals, birds, fish, insects, mythical creatures, and abstract designs.

Petroglyphs like this one at the Three Rivers site may depict imaginary or mythical animals.

31 Did they do other kinds of artwork?

Yes, they painted pictures on the surface of rocks or pecked them using stone hammers and chisels. Painted pictures are called *pictographs*, while pecked ones are called *petroglyphs*. You can see lots of petroglyphs in New Mexico at Three Rivers Petroglyph National Recreational Site and Petroglyph National Monument.

This pictograph in Hueco Tanks State Historical Park near El Paso, Texas, was painted by Mogollon Indians 600 to 800 years ago.

32 How did these ancient Indians make paint?

They ground up colors, or pigments, from certain clays and minerals. For example, they made white pigment from gypsum, red from hematite, and black from charcoal. Artists still draw with charcoal today.

Once they had the desired pigment, they needed a binder (gooey stuff to make the paint stick). Egg whites, pine gum, and the juice of yucca plants made good binders. To make the paint flow, artists added water to the mixture. They could apply paint with their fingers, blow it through hollow reeds, or use brushes made from plant fibers.

33 How did the Mogollon get their name?

We're not sure what prehistoric Indians called themselves. So, archeologists decided to name the Mogollon after the mountains in New Mexico where they first found the remains of their settlements. The mountains are named after Don Juan Ignacio Flores Mogollon, who was governor of New Mexico in the early 1700s.

34 Do the Mogollon Indians have descendants today?

Yes, but it's not clear where the Mogollon went when they left their old homes. Some may have moved to the middle Rio Grande region. The Zuni, Hopi, and Ácoma Indians may have Mogollon ancestors.

Mortar and pestle used to pound colored minerals into paint pigments

35 What about the Hohokam, where did they live?

In the Sonoran Desert in southern Arizona. Even though the region receives little rainfall and summer temperatures soar to over 100 degrees, the Hohokam thrived there for centuries.

In spring, the Hohokam ate buds of the cholla cactus, *foreground,* and in summer they collected fruit from the saguaro cactus, *distance.* The wooden ribs of the saguaro also made a good building material.

36 How did they survive in the hot desert?

Even in that severe environment, they were able to find food, water, and shelter. For food, they gathered beans from the mesquite tree, hearts from the agave, fruit from cacti, and seeds from wild plants. They made medicinal teas from the creosote bush to treat illnesses. They built their homes using ocotillo and saguaro ribs.

The baked hearts of the agave also were a favorite food.

In late summer, the Hohokam gathered mesquite beans, which they pounded into meal or stored in baskets.

39 Why did they build canals?

The canals carried water to their fields of corn, squash, beans, and cotton. Believe it or not, their main canals were nearly six feet deep and more than fifty feet wide! They dug more than five hundred miles of main canals in the Salt River Valley around Phoenix.

37 What is culture?

It's everything about what groups of people are like and how they live. Let's say you are telling a friend about what people are like in a certain country. You tell her about the food they eat, the language they speak, the clothes they wear, the art they make, the games they play and the religious beliefs they have. What you're describing is their culture.

Archeologist Emil Haury standing in an excavated Hohokam canal in 1964. Some ancient canals were redug and modernized in modern times and are still in use.

38 What was Hohokam culture like?

Well, one thing the Hohokam are known for are the hundreds of miles of canals they built. They lived along large rivers such as the Salt and Gila (HEE-la), which flow out of the mountains near Phoenix.

40 Why did the Hohokam gather wild plants when they had gardens?

Why not? Wild food is good to eat and you can't always count on farming. What if a drought strikes and rivers dry up? What if floods destroy the irrigation canals? When you think about it, hunting and gathering are more reliable than agriculture. Indians living in the Sonoran Desert today still gather some native plants for food.

Juanita Ahil, a Tohono O'odham woman, uses a long pole to pick saguaro cactus fruit.

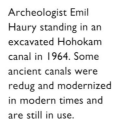

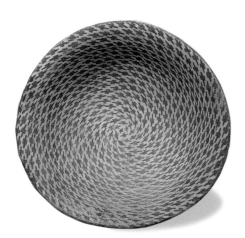

Finely decorated Hohokam pottery bowl made more than 900 years ago

41 What did the Hohokam do for fun?

Some of the same things we do. They danced, played with toys, made music, and competed in a special kind of ball game.

This pottery figurine of an animal may have been a child's toy.

A Hohokam person made this petroglyph of dancers.

42 What kind of ball game?

We're not sure what the rules were, but it took place in a large oval court surrounded by embankments. Spectators lined the banks to watch while teams tried to knock a ball in a goal or through a hoop. Unlike modern American games, the Hohokam ball game seems to have combined a sporting event with a religious ritual.

You can see this ballcourt at Wupatki National Monument near Flagstaff, Arizona.

43 Was the ball they used like a basketball?

More like a baseball. In 1909, a rubber ball that might have been used in their games was discovered at a site in Arizona. The ball was more than eight hundred years old.

This ball made of stone may have been used in some kind of Hohokam game.

44 How do you know for sure what the Hohokam did?

We don't, but archeological excavations produce many clues about the past and the descendants of the Hohokam tell us a lot about how their ancestors lived.

45 How far back in time would I have to go to meet a Hohokam?

More than five hundred years. But Hohokam Indians lived in what is now southern Arizona for a thousand years before then.

Hohokam petroglyphs in Saguaro National Park near Tucson, Arizona.

46 If I could go back in time, what would I see there?

That depends. If you were to visit a Hohokam village of eight hundred years ago, you'd see a bustling community of people living in clusters of houses enclosed by an adobe (dried mud) wall. In the middle of town you would find a huge flat-topped mound of earth with colorfully painted houses on top and a ball court nearby.

47 Who lived up on the mounds?

Probably people with influence in the community such as religious leaders or wealthy corn and cotton merchants. Archeologists believe these individuals wore finely woven robes, exotic mosaic jewelry, decorated shell pendants, and colored feathers in their hair. Because some of the mounds are over twenty feet high, they would have been impressive places for village leaders to hold ceremonies or show off their power.

48 What was Hohokam jewelry like?

Gorgeous! Their favorite material was shell, which traders brought all the way from the Gulf of California or the Pacific Coast more than two hundred miles away! They made shell pendants with etched designs to hang around their necks. They also cut turquoise into small geometric pieces and glued them into mosaics of frogs and birds onto the shell's surface.

The Hohokam made beads, rings, bracelets, hair pins, and plugs to put in their ears and noses. They painted their bodies in bright colors and wore feathered headdresses. They even made mirrors from pieces of polished pyrite, which also is called "fool's gold."

Top to bottom: slate bird pendant; shell bracelet; shell bird fetishes; carved sea shell with horned lizard design; shell necklace; shell mosaic bird pendant; stone paint palette.

49 Did the Hohokam have stores?

They probably had trade fairs like our county fairs. These may have been scheduled to coincide with religious festivals and ball games. Traders would come from all around to sell pottery, jewelry, mosaics, paint palettes, mirrors, rare stones, carved effigies of animals, finely woven cotton cloths, copper bells and parrot feathers from Mexico, and sea shells.

Today the ruins of Casa Grande are protected from the weather by a roof.

50 Can we visit any Hohokam villages today?

Yes, but only a few. One is Pueblo Grande in Phoenix, Arizona, and another is Casa Grande Ruins National Monument in Coolidge, Arizona. Built in the early 1300s, Casa Grande's walls are four stories high and four feet thick at the base, and made of caliche-adobe. Caliche is a hard whitish soil (calcium carbonate) that accumulates in layers underground. Adobe consists mostly of clay. The Hohokam mixed these materials with water to make a stiff mud that they laid down in layers to build walls. When the mud dried, it hardened like a brick.

51 Why are there so few Hohokam sites?

Many were destroyed by modern development, such as plowing land for agriculture and building cities and highways. Did you know that the remains of at least fifty Hohokam villages lie under Phoenix?

Another problem is looting. Looters sneak out to ruins to dig up artifacts to sell. It is illegal to do this on public land such as national forests and parks. Often, pottery and other valuable artifacts are found in human graves. When looters dig these things up, they disturb sacred burials, which deeply offends everyone.

Archeological sites are like libraries. They contain a wealth of information about how people lived in ancient times. After looters damage a site, that information is lost forever.

Examples of Hohokam redware pottery

52 What happened to the Hohokam?

Nobody's quite sure. Floods may have ruined their canals and farmlands, or civil war may have destroyed their towns. Hohokam culture ended but the Hohokam people survived.

When Spaniards explored Arizona in the 1600s, they found the ball courts and mounds of the Hohokam overgrown and their houses melted into the desert. They also found Pima and Tohono O'odham Indians living in the old Hohokam homeland.

53 Did the Hohokam ever meet Mogollon or Anasazi people?

Sure, plenty of times. The Hohokam often traveled into Mogollon and Anasazi lands. It was easier to visit and trade with them than to travel to Mexico and California.

Other folks they met were the Salado Indians, who are named after the *Rio Salado*, the Salt River. Scholars don't know too much about the Salado and don't always agree on where they came from or who they were, or even if they were a distinct culture. Some of their customs were similar to those of the Hohokam, but in other ways they resembled the Mogollon and Anasazi. Nevertheless, the Salado are known for their beautiful pottery, which has finely painted black and white designs on a reddish background.

A Salado jar

Reconstructed room at Besh-Ba-Gowah Archaeological Park in Globe, Arizona

54 When did the Salado live?

Between around A.D. 1100 and 1450. Of course, they had ancestors who lived before then and descendants who came afterwards, but 1100 to 1450 is the period when they made pottery, stone tools, and architecture in a distinctive style that archeologists have named "Salado."

55 Did they also live in the desert?

Yes, but at a slightly higher elevation. They lived around where Roosevelt Reservoir and Globe, Arizona are today. In 1911, when the Salt River was dammed, many Salado villages were flooded. Among those to remain above water were cliff dwellings in Tonto National Monument and the village of Besh-Ba-Gowah. When archeologists uncovered one room at Besh-Ba-Gowah, they discovered an altar and a hole in the floor filled with turquoise and sealed with a large quartz crystal.

Cliff dwelling at Tonto National Monument, Arizona

Adolph Bandelier

56 How did archeologists learn about the Salado?

An explorer named Adolph F. Bandelier roamed the Salado area in 1883 and recorded his findings. Bandelier was born in Switzerland in 1840 and moved to America as a child. He spent most of his life studying American Indian cultures. He trekked great distances throughout the Southwest, mostly on foot, covering as much as fifty miles in one day. As he went, he recorded ruins and talked with Native American people about their history and customs. Bandelier National Monument in New Mexico, which has hundreds of prehistoric Indian cave dwellings, is named after this anthropologist.

57 Were there other cultures in Arizona during ancient times?

Yes, the Sinagua. They appeared around 1300 years ago and thrived for about 600 years. In Spanish, *sin* means "without" and *agua* means "water." Harold S. Colton, the scientist who identified this culture, called them Sinagua when he noticed how arid the country was around some of their sites.

Many Sinagua lived in northern Arizona and some lived a little further south in the Verde Valley.

Sunset Crater is quiet now.

58 What was life like for the Sinagua?

In 1064, a volcano called Sunset Crater began a series of eruptions that continued for two hundred years and spread a blanket of cinders and ashes over eight hundred square miles. Even today, much of the land looks like a black desert. Many Sinagua homes were buried, but fortunately the volcano rumbled and smoked before erupting, giving the Indians time to save their lives.

59 What happened after the volcano erupted?

The Sinagua eventually moved back. They found that the blanket of fine cinders on the surface of the ground was beneficial to farming. The ash, which was only a few inches deep in many places, acted as a mulch to conserve precious moisture.

60 Why did Sunset Crater erupt?

The Hopi Indians have a legend to explain its eruption. It is a story about a Hopi maiden who long ago married a *kachina*, a supernatural being. At first, they lived together happily but then the kachina became angry at certain people in his wife's village because of an evil thing they had done. To scare them, he lit a huge bonfire on a hill where Sunset Crater is today. This bonfire soon got out of control and burned a hole deep into the ground. The hole finally connected to the molten lava that lies way below the surface of the earth. Then fire, smoke, lava, and ashes erupted out of the hole and formed the volcano.

This Hopi figurine represents Kana'a, the friendly spirit living on Sunset Crater.

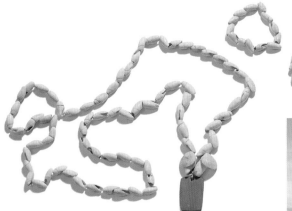

This shell necklace and matching bracelets once belonged to a Sinagua Indian.

61 What were Sinagua houses like?

Early on, like so many southwestern people, they lived in pit houses. However, around 900 years ago they began constructing remarkable castle-like buildings such as Wupatki and Wukoki. They also built cliff dwellings like Montezuma Castle and hilltop villages like Tuzigoot in Arizona. Montezuma Castle is tucked into a cave so high up in a cliff that you wonder how its residents reached it.

Wukoki Pueblo ruins at Wupatki National Monument

Lomaki Ruin at Wupatki

62 Do Sinagua Indians still live around Flagstaff?

No and yes. The "no" part is that the Sinagua left their homeland in the 1300s. Many moved east to join the Hopi. Members of some Hopi clans believe their ancestors once lived in certain Sinagua pueblos. The "yes" part is that today many Hopi Indians live and work in Flagstaff.

63 How can you tell when things happened in the past?

One way is by a process called tree-ring dating. Some species of southwestern trees live for centuries and each year they grow a new layer of wood around their trunks. In rainy years, these layers or "rings" are thick; in dry years they're thin. Together, these rings show a pattern of growth.

To determine the date of an old house, you first take cross-section samples from some of its roof beams. Then you measure and count the annual growth rings. Now you can figure out what year the tree was chopped down – that's probably the same year it was used to build the house.

The broken roof beam shown here would reveal annual growth rings. Notice how the ceiling was built.

Archeologists recovered these scrapers from Pueblo Bonito in Chaco Canyon. They are made of deer bone with inlaid jet and turquoise.

Faces chipped into rock by ancient Puebloans

64 What about the Anasazi?

They also were southwestern farmers and they are the ancestors of today's Pueblo Indians, who live in New Mexico and Arizona. Anasazi culture began 2,500 or more years ago and lasted for at least 2,000 years. Originally, these Indians made their homes in the Four Corners region (where the states of Arizona, Utah, Colorado, and New Mexico meet), but later they spread over most of the Southwest.

The Anasazi often painted handprints like these on canyon walls.

Pueblo Bonito, at Chaco Culture National Historical Park in New Mexico, is famous for its massive construction and fine stonework.

65 Why are they called Anasazi?

It's a term the Navajo Indians used to refer to the ancient people whose villages are found in their land. Navajos told archeologists that the former inhabitants of these sites were *Anasazi* and the word soon became common usage. The Pueblo Indians, however, have their own names for their ancestors. For example, the Hopi call them the *Hisatsinom*. Today, some people say "Pueblo ancestors" instead of Anasazi.

67 What did the Anasazi call themselves?

We don't know. They probably spoke different languages, which are reflected in the variety of languages spoken today by the Pueblo Indians. Most Native Americans' names for themselves mean "the People."

66 Did any other Indians get the wrong name?

Yes. *Navajo* is a word from one of the Pueblo languages. Navajos call themselves *Dineh* (Di-NEY). The Tohono O'odham people, who live in southern Arizona, used to be called Papagos, which is a Pima Indian word. And don't forget, even the word "Indian" is wrong – some Indians prefer "Native American."

68 How were the Pueblo ancestors' lives different from the Hohokam's?

For one thing, they lived up on the Colorado Plateau, which has cooler and wetter weather. With more rain, they could grow corn, beans, and squash without digging large irrigation systems. They had lots of wood to use for fuel and house-building, and there was plenty of game to hunt, such as deer, elk, bighorn sheep, and rabbits.

Cliff house at Mesa Verde National Park in Colorado. Notice the kiva entrances in the plaza.

69 What were their houses like?

They were sturdy ground-level structures with solid stone or adobe walls and ceilings of wood timbers overlaid with grass and dirt. They often dug a *kiva* (a circular room built into the ground) in the plaza as a gathering place for members of the pueblo.

How many kivas can you find in this view of Pueblo Bonito?

70 Why were kivas underground?

Partly for religious reasons. The idea of Mother Earth, who nurtures life, is very important in Pueblo religion. Traditional Pueblo Indians believe that long ago their ancestors came up into this world from another world below. According to their beliefs, people emerged into the present world through a hole in the earth. The Hopis and Zunis believe this hole, or place of emergence, is in the Grand Canyon.

When archeologists excavate kivas, they often find a small hole in the floor, which represents the place of emergence. Sometimes this hole, which Hopis call the *sipapu*, contains a sacred object such as a tiny pot or piece of jewelry.

71 What was a kiva like inside?

Some kivas were large, others small, depending on how many people were to use them. Most were round and had a firepit in the middle of the floor. Fresh air came in through a vent along the floor and smoke from the fire rose up through a hatch in the ceiling.

People entered kivas by a ladder through the hatch. During a meeting or ceremony, they sat in a circle around the floor. Many kivas had sitting benches or shelves around the edges and wall niches to hold ritual objects. They often had looms, too, that were used for weaving fabrics.

Archeologists rebuilt this very large kiva at Aztec Ruins National Monument in New Mexico to show how it looked hundreds of years ago.

72 Why did they build some houses in cliffs?

Probably for protection from invaders and for shelter from the wind and rain. Being dry, cliff houses were perfect places to store food. They nearly always faced south and thus were warmed by the sun in winter.

Cliff Palace at Mesa Verde, the largest cliff dwelling in the Southwest

The Anasazi cut these steps in the side of a cliff along the San Juan River.

73 How did they climb in and out of their cliff homes?

Very carefully! They used ladders made from logs and chipped niches called "hand-and-toe holds" in the cliff walls. They probably used ropes, too, woven from yucca fibers.

74 Did everyone live in cliff dwellings?

No. Most villages were out in the open. Even at Mesa Verde, which is famous for its cliff dwellings, most people lived on the open mesas. Thousands more people lived in large towns in the Montezuma Valley below Mesa Verde. You can see impressive village remains at Hovenweep National Monument and Chaco Culture National Historical Park.

Corrugated jars such as this one often were used for cooking.

Pueblo Bonito
from the air

75 What are some of the prehistoric Pueblo sites?

The largest cliff dwelling is Cliff Palace in Mesa Verde National Park. It has two hundred rooms. Another very large pueblo is at Aztec Ruins National Monument, where you can walk through many rooms and a huge reconstructed kiva. But, the most famous site is Pueblo Bonito in Chaco Culture National Historical Park. It has more than six hundred fifty rooms and forty kivas and parts of it once stood five stories high.

Betatakin, a group of ancient dwellings in Navajo National Monument, Arizona

White House ruins
in Canyon de Chelly

76 Did Anasazi homes have kitchens?

Each home had a cooking area with a fire pit and various cooking utensils. People would set their cooking pots on three stones (called firedogs) on the hearth. They had flat polished-stone griddles on which they baked *piki* bread, which looks like large thin tortillas or wafers. To bake corn and other foods, they dug ovens in the earth and lined them with stones.

This beautifully decorated ceramic dipper may have been used to ladle water from a jar.

Rolled up piki bread Piki is made from a thin batter of finely ground cornmeal, which is baked on a hot stone griddle.

Ceramic bowls and mugs were common Anasazi housewares.

Ancient Puebloans once used pits like this to cook food. First they would make a fire in the pit to heat up the stone lining. Then they would lay in yucca fruit or other food to roast.

The Anasazi made pottery by hand and most modern Pueblo potters still do it this way.

77 How did they make pots?

Pots are made from clay, a fine-grained mineral found in the ground. A potter would bring some raw clay home and painstakingly clean and prepare it for making pottery. When the clay was ready, she would coil it to form bowls, jars, and mugs. When these dried, she would polish them with a smooth stone and sometimes paint a design on the surface. The final step was to bake them in a fire. When clay reaches a high temperature it turns into ceramic, which is hard like stone.

The Pueblo ancestors used ceramic pots to hold water, store grain, and cook food. Like the Hohokam, they excelled at making pottery and traded it widely. Each local group developed its own distinctive style. As you might guess, learning the different pottery styles is part of every archeologist's education.

78 Who made pottery?

Girls and women. When a person died, he or she often was buried with some of their favorite personal possessions to accompany them to the next world. Since pottery-making tools have been found in the graves of women, we assume women were the potters.

Even today, it is mostly Pueblo women who make pottery. Two famous Pueblo potters of the twentieth century were Nampeyo, from Tewa Village, and Maria Martínez, from San Ildefonso Pueblo.

Prairie dogs are rodents that live in underground burrows and often sit on mounds by their holes watching for predators.

79 What did the Pueblo ancestors eat?

Lots of corn as well as squash and beans. They also ate native plants such as goosefoot, pigweed, purslane, and sunflowers, all of which grew between the rows or along the borders of cultivated fields. Of course, like all southwestern Indians, they ate the meat of many animals – deer and antelope, rabbits and prairie dogs, turkeys and ducks, and even mice, just to name a few.

Seeds from sunflowers and native grasses formed part of ancient Indians' diet.

After much use, the mano wore a deep groove in the metate.

80 How did they make cornmeal?

With grinding tools we call *manos* and *metates*. A metate is a large stone with a flat surface. You place corn kernels, seeds, or nuts on it and grind them into meal using a smaller hand stone, or mano (which means *hand* in Spanish).

81 What might they have had for dinner?

Rabbit stew. They might boil the meat in a pot with wild onions, purslane, herbs, and cornmeal.

Then they might enjoy some baked chokecherry cakes with honey dribbled on top, or fresh banana yucca fruit. After dessert they'd sit and enjoy mugs of hot tea flavored with mint leaves.

Potsherds are the most abundant artifacts found in archeological sites. Notice all the different styles in this picture. Hundreds of years ago, corncobs were smaller than they are today.

What kind of animals do you think these petroglyphs show?

Indians made different types of arrows and arrowheads to use when hunting different sized game such as birds or bighorn sheep.

82 How did the Indian ancestors catch rabbits?

One way was in a rabbit drive. Friends and neighbors would quietly form a large circle around a field. Everyone would start clapping their hands, shouting, and stomping around to flush out the little animals. Then they'd close the circle, catch the rabbits in the middle, and club them. Of course, they'd catch rabbits individually, too, by setting traps and nets along their trails.

Jackrabbits are common in the Southwest.

83 Did they have pets?

They had dogs, but dogs were probably not household pets as we think of them today. Dogs helped keep villages clean by eating scraps of food and warned of a stranger's approach by barking. Hunters may have used dogs to help run down game, and resourceful weavers spun dog hair into yarn.

Small carving of a dog

These upright sticks are the remains of an Anasazi turkey pen.

84 Did they raise animals, like cows and chickens?

Cows and chickens didn't exist in the Southwest then, but they did raise turkeys. Archeologists have found remains of turkey pens along the edge of village plazas, sometimes even including nests with eggs in them. They had parrots, too, especially scarlet macaws, which were brought up by traders from Mexico. Indians still use these colorful feathers to adorn costumes and headdresses for ceremonies.

Feathers from a scarlet macaw

A wild turkey

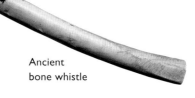

Ancient
bone whistle

85 How about music?

They sang songs and played instruments
such as flutes, drums, and rattles. They made flutes
from hollow reeds or the leg bones of turkeys and
eagles, and rattles from deer hooves tied together.
They also had a sound-maker called a bull roarer,
often made from a flat animal bone loosely wrapped
in deer hide. They tied one end of a long string to
the bone and the other end to a wood handle.
They'd swing the bone round and round in the air
to produce a strange whirring, moaning sound.

Petroglyph of a flute
player in Monument
Valley. Is he carrying
a pack on his back?

86 Did kids go to school?

Yes and no. School is where you learn
things to help you in life. For example,
today we learn how to read and write and
operate computers. In the past, Indian
children learned other skills – which wild
plants to eat and which to avoid, how to
make spearpoints, how to sew clothes and
weave blankets. Their teachers were parents,
grandparents, and other adults.

87 Did southwestern Indians have a calendar?

They marked the seasons by watching the sun. As the sun passes
overhead, it casts shadows that help tell the time of day. They
determined dates by noticing the position of the sun in relation
to visible marks on the horizon, such as a hilltop behind which
the sun rose in the morning or set in the evening. Two important dates each year were the summer solstice (around June 21)
and the winter solstice (around December 21).

These large figures were
pecked on a cliff along the San
Juan River about 2,000 years
ago. Notice their headdresses,
beaded necklaces, fringed belts,
and big dangling feet. They may
represent supernatural beings.

88 Who was in charge of the villages?

Religious leaders planned ceremonies and rituals to help bring harmony in nature and
success in farming. Everyone knew how important it was to maintain good relationships
with the supernatural beings who could send rain and fertility. The Hopi Indians,
many of whose traditions go back to their Pueblo ancestors, call their village leader the
kikmongwi. This individual has much respect and authority and is expected to use these
privileges for everyone's benefit.

89 What kind of clothes did they wear?

They made shirts, pants, and moccasins from softened deer skin and wove breechclouts, shawls, and blankets from cotton. They used animal hair to weave belts and sashes and used yucca fibers to make sandals. To keep warm in winter, they made blankets and robes out of turkey feathers and rabbit fur.

Anasazi sandals woven out of yucca, *above*, and cordage, *right*

This Hopi woman is modeling a turkey-feather cape.

90 How did they weave turkey feathers?

First they would make some string from twisted yucca fibers and collect lots of small turkey breast feathers. They'd loosen a twist in the string, stick in a feather, loosen another twist and stick in another feather, and keep doing that until the string was full of feathers. Then they would sew the strings of feathers together.

91 What was the most useful plant?

Indians used many plants to meet many different needs, but yucca may have been the most versatile. They used its fibers to make paint brushes, sandals, and mats; they made soap from its roots; they ate its fruit and added the blossoms to their salads; and they used its juice as a binder for paint.

Flowering yucca plant

92 Did they play games like the Hohokam?

They didn't have ball courts, but kids used to toss shuttlecocks through hoops. Shuttlecocks were like darts, made by sticking a turkey feather into the end of a corncob. The hoops were about a foot in diameter, woven out of grasses and sticks. One player would toss a hoop in the air while another would try to throw the shuttlecock through its hole.

93 How did they pay for food or clothing?

Instead of using money, they traded. If your dad had extra corn but needed cotton to make clothes, he'd trade his surplus corn with someone else for their surplus cotton. Sometimes people would travel to distant communities to trade their wares.

When it was excavated from a ruin, this ancient Anasazi basket contained objects used by a medicine man for healing.

94 Did ancient Indians smoke cigarettes?

Yes. Tobacco was a native plant. They smoked reed cigarettes, puffed on clay pipes, and chewed pieces of tobacco and lime wrapped in yucca leaves. But, they didn't smoke casually, like people do today. More likely, they smoked during rituals.

95 What if kids got sick, were there doctors?

Sure, but not like modern doctors. Medicine men and women knew the healing arts and used various herbs to treat illnesses. For example, milkweed tea was a remedy for stomach troubles. And, did you know that aspirin originally was made from willow bark?

96 What kind of art did ancestral Pueblo people make?

Fine baskets, embroidered cotton cloth, exquisite jewelry, and beautiful pottery. In addition, the Pueblo ancestors left thousands of examples of rock art – pictures of animals, birds, snakes, people, and mythological creatures.

ctographs of animals in Painted Cave, andelier National Monument, New Mexico

Turquoise beaded necklace, woven basket

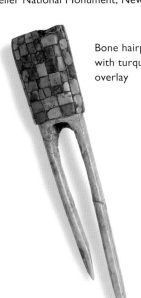

Bone hairpin with turquoise overlay

Jet frog

Portion of a large petroglyph panel called "Newspaper Rock" in eastern Utah

97 What happened to the people who lived at Mesa Verde and Chaco?

Archeologists think droughts in the 1200s may have caused severe food shortages, resulting in starvation and disease. There also may have been warfare. For whatever reason, by 1300 nearly everyone had decided to seek a better life elsewhere.

98 Where did they go?

Lots of different places. Some Pueblo Indians in Northern New Mexico trace their past to Mesa Verde. Many Ácoma people, on the other hand, believe their ancestors came from Chaco Canyon.

All Pueblo Indians tell about a time of migration in their distant past. They say their ancestors wandered around the Southwest looking for a permanent home. They settled for a while in certain locations where we find ruins and cliff dwellings today. Some of these places are in our national parks and monuments. Eventually, each group found its new homeland.

Ácoma Pueblo, built in the 1200s, sits atop a high mesa in New Mexico. Ácoma Pueblo Indians still live there.

At Pecos, a kiva and a Spanish church are next to each other.

99 How did their lives change?

For three more centuries, they continued to thrive as farmers. Many groups had their villages in the Rio Grande valley where Spanish explorers encountered them in 1540. The Spaniards met many Pueblo Indian groups – the Zuni, Hopi, Jémez, Pecos, and others.

When Southwestern Indians came into contact with the Spaniards, their lives changed drastically. Thousands died from European diseases to which they had little resistance. The Spaniards forced them to work on ranches and in mines and forbade them to practice their own religion. Some Indians over time adapted to the new influences by acquiring horses and sheep, cultivating new crops, marrying Spaniards, and even practicing Spanish customs.

You can see evidence of these two cultures by visiting places such as Pecos National Historical Park in New Mexico.

100 What other Indians live in the Southwest today?

Two large groups are the Navajos and Apaches whose ancestors migrated to the Southwest long ago from Canada. The Utes and Paiutes, who were nomadic hunter-gatherers in ancient times, also live in the Southwest.

The Pima, Tohono O'odham, and Maricopa Indians have reservations in southern Arizona. Some members of these groups trace their ancestry to the Hohokam. The Yavapai and Hualapai live in central Arizona and the Havasupai have their homes within the Grand Canyon. All these people say they have always lived in the Southwest. More recent arrivals, however, are the Yaqui Indians who live around Phoenix and Tucson. They came to Arizona as refugees from Mexico in the early 1900s.

| 0 | Do Native Americans today still follow the ways of their ancestors?

To some extent. Many still speak their native languages. This is especially true of older adults. But, because English is the dominant language of our society, fewer children are learning to speak their native languages.

Many southwestern Indians practice their religion, and Pueblo people still hold ceremonies in kivas and in village plazas. However, outsiders may only attend if invited. Religious leaders teach traditional values concerning how their people should live and behave and how they should treat the land that nurtures us.

Native American artists and writers continue to express their rich cultural heritage through their art: pottery, jewelry, basketry, paintings, sculpture, literature, and dance. The Mogollon, Hohokam, Salado, Sinagua, and Anasazi lived a long time ago, but their culture didn't vanish, it simply changed with time.

Modern Indians of the Southwest are the descendants of Indians who lived here centuries ago. *Clockwise from top left:* Elnora Malpatis, a Hualapai basketmaker from Peach Springs, Arizona; Ivan Lewis, a potter from Cochiti Pueblo, New Mexico; two girls from Santa Clara Pueblo, New Mexico; and a boy from San Juan Pueblo in his Comanche Dance costume.

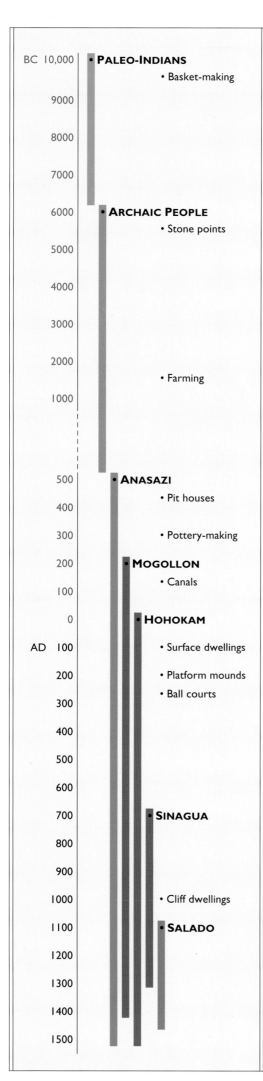

BC 10,000	**PALEO-INDIANS**
	• Basket-making
9000	
8000	
7000	
6000	**ARCHAIC PEOPLE**
5000	• Stone points
4000	
3000	
2000	
1000	• Farming
500	**ANASAZI**
400	• Pit houses
300	• Pottery-making
200	**MOGOLLON**
100	• Canals
0	**HOHOKAM**
AD 100	• Surface dwellings
200	• Platform mounds
300	• Ball courts
400	
500	
600	
700	**SINAGUA**
800	
900	
1000	• Cliff dwellings
1100	**SALADO**
1200	
1300	
1400	
1500	

Published by Southwest Parks and Monuments Association
221 North Court, Tucson, Arizona 85701

Net proceeds from SPMA publications support educational and research programs in the National Park Service.

Library of Congress Cataloging-in-Publication Data
Noble, David Grant.
101 questions about ancient Indians of the Southwest / by David Grant Noble.
p. cm.
Summary: Surveys of the history, culture and lifestyles of the ancient Indians of the Southwest through 101 questions.
ISBN 1-877856-87-8
1. Indians of North America – Southwest, New – Miscellanea – Juvenile literature.   2. Indians of North America –
Southwest, New – Social life and customs – Juvenile literature.   3. Questions and answers – Juvenile literature.
[1. Indians of North America – Southwest, New – Miscellanea.   2. Questions and answers.]   I. Title.
E78.S7N625   1998
979'.00497 – dc21
97-53261   CIP   AC

Editing: Laura Symms Wallace
Design: Rebecca Livermore
Illustrations: Richard Lang, page 3; Brian Wignall, page 11; Lawrence Ormsby, page 14
Maps: Deborah Reade, pages 2 and 8; *Time line:* Rebecca Livermore

Photography: **front cover:** *Arrow in straightening shaft, Mimbres polychrome bowl, Sinagua stone knife, Hohokam carved stone vessel
with pigment, Archaic split twig figure and Hohokam pottery face:* Jerry Jacka; *Anasazi jet frog, turquoise necklace, deer bone scraper and bear
shaman petroglyph:* George H. H. Huey; *Anasazi sandal and Anasazi polychrome ladle:* Chuck Place; **page 1:** *Anasazi painted clay
figurine:* Jerry Jacka; **page 3:** *Forest:* Stephen Trimble; *Fossil:* Larry D. Agenbroad; **page 4:** *Tom Toslino:* Denver Public Library,
Western History Department; *Spear points:* Jerry Jacka; *George McJunkin:* Museum of New Mexico; **page 5:** *Petrified forest:*
Tom Till; *Paiute Indians:* Museum of New Mexico; *Stone pestle:* Helga Teiwes; **page 6:** *Prickly pear:* Peter Kresan; *Pine nuts:*
Stephen Trimble; *Rainbow grasshopper:* John Cancalosi; *Antelope ground squirrel:* Shirley Berquist; **page 7:** *Lithic scatter:*
Stephen Trimble; *Basket:* George H. H. Huey; *Great Gallery mural:* Tom Danielsen; **page 8:** *Farmer:* Stephen Trimble;
Corn cobs: Michael Collier; **page 9:** *Stone tools:* Jerry Jacka; *Human hair net:* Douglas Kahn; *Pit house:* George H. H. Huey;
page 10: *Mimbres butterfly and fish bowls:* Jerry Jacka; *Mimbres antelope bowl:* Chuck Place; *Petroglyph and pictograph:*
Laurence Parent; **page 11:** *Stone vessels and pigments:* Jerry Jacka; *Sonoran desert:* George H. H. Huey; *Agave:* Jeff Gnass;
page 12: *Bowl:* Jerry Jacka; *Canal* (courtesy Arizona State Museum): Helga Teiwes; *Juanita Ahil:* Thomas A. Wiewandt;
page 13: *Clay figure:* Larry Lindahl; *Petroglyph dancers:* Jerry Jacka; *Ball court:* Randy A. Prentice; *Ball* (courtesy Arizona State
Museum): Ken Matesich; **page 14:** *Petroglyphs:* Laurence Parent; **page 15:** *Jewelry and decorative objects:* Jerry Jacka;
page 16: *Casa Grande:* George H. H. Huey; *Redware pottery:* Jerry Jacka; **page 17:** *Polychrome pottery and Besh-Ba-Gowah:*
Jerry Jacka; *Tonto National Monument:* George H. H. Huey; *Adolph Bandelier:* National Park Service; **page 18:** *Sunset Crater
and kachina:* George H. H. Huey; **page 19:** *Shell necklace and roof beams:* George H. H. Huey; *Wukoki ruin:* Patrick Fischer;
Lomaki ruin: Tom Till; **page 20:** *Deer bone scraper and Pueblo Bonito doorways:* George H. H. Huey; *Faces petroglyphs:* David Noble;
Handprint pictographs: Tom Danielsen; **page 21:** *Spruce Tree House:* Chuck Place; *Pueblo Bonito kivas and Aztec Ruins kiva interior:*
George H. H. Huey; **page 22:** *Mesa Verde:* Tom Till; *Steps:* Peter Kresan; *Ladder and corrugated jar:* George H. H. Huey;
page 23: *Chaco Canyon:* Tom Till; *Betatakin and White House ruins:* George H. H. Huey; **page 24:** *Polychrome ladle:* Chuck Place;
Stone oven: Stephen Post; *Hopi potters hands and piki bread:* Stephen Trimble; *Polychrome bowl and black-on-white mug:*
George H. H. Huey; **page 25:** *Pueblo garden:* Stephen Trimble; *Prairie dog:* Paul and Shirley Berquist; *Mano and metate and
arrows:* Jerry Jacka; *Antelope petroglyph:* Tom Danielsen; *Pottery sherds:* Larry Ulrich; **page 26:** *Blacktail jackrabbit:* Tom Bean;
Dog fetish: Jerry Jacka; *Turkey pen ruin:* Peter Kresan; *Macaw feathers:* George H. H. Huey; *Wild turkey:* Stephen Trimble;
page 27: *Kokopelli and whistle:* Jerry Jacka; *San Juan River petroglyphs:* Larry Ulrich; **page 28:** *Anasazi sandals:* Chuck Place;
Turkey feather robe: Dewitt Jones; *Banana yucca:* Steve Mulligan; **page 29:** *Shaman's basket and bone hair pin:* Jerry Jacka;
Bandelier pictographs, turquoise necklace and jet frog: George H. H. Huey; *Round basket:* Chuck Place; *Newspaper Rock:* Jeff Gnass;
page 30: *Ácoma Pueblo:* Stephen Trimble; *Pecos National Monument:* David Muench; **page 31:** *Four Native American
portraits:* Stephen Trimble; *Effigy pottery vessel:* George H. H. Huey; **back cover:** *Anasazi hand print:* David Noble.

Prepress color preparation: Hollis Digital Imaging, Inc.
Printing: Lorraine Press
Printed on recycled paper with inks from renewable resources